Contents

Section 1

Course Planning

Student

Year

COURSES

Course Planning

Student

Year

COURSES

Course Planning

Student

Year

COURSES

Course Planning

Student

Year

COURSES

Homeschool Curriculum Purchases

Resource	Where to Purchase	Cost

Gratitude List

I'M THANKFUL FOR:

Thoughts

NOTES

Homeschool Day

Attendance Record

Year ______________________

Jan	1	2	3	4	5	6	7	8	9	10	11	12	13	14	15	16	17
	18	19	20	21	22	23	24	25	26	27	28	29	30	31			
Feb	1	2	3	4	5	6	7	8	9	10	11	12	13	14	15	16	17
	18	19	20	21	22	23	24	25	26	27	28	29					
March	1	2	3	4	5	6	7	8	9	10	11	12	13	14	15	16	17
	18	19	20	21	22	23	24	25	26	27	28	29	30	31			
April	1	2	3	4	5	6	7	8	9	10	11	12	13	14	15	16	17
	18	19	20	21	22	23	24	25	26	27	28	29	30				
May	1	2	3	4	5	6	7	8	9	10	11	12	13	14	15	16	17
	18	19	20	21	22	23	24	25	26	27	28	29	30	31			
June	1	2	3	4	5	6	7	8	9	10	11	12	13	14	15	16	17
	18	19	20	21	22	23	24	25	26	27	28	29	30				

Homeschool Day

Attendance Record

Year ______________________

Month																	
July	1	2	3	4	5	6	7	8	9	10	11	12	13	14	15	16	17
	18	19	20	21	22	23	24	25	26	27	28	29	30	31			
Aug	1	2	3	4	5	6	7	8	9	10	11	12	13	14	15	16	17
	18	19	20	21	22	23	24	25	26	27	28	29	30	31			
Sept	1	2	3	4	5	6	7	8	9	10	11	12	13	14	15	16	17
	18	19	20	21	22	23	24	25	26	27	28	29	30				
Oct	1	2	3	4	5	6	7	8	9	10	11	12	13	14	15	16	17
	18	19	20	21	22	23	24	25	26	27	28	29	30	31			
Nov	1	2	3	4	5	6	7	8	9	10	11	12	13	14	15	16	17
	18	19	20	21	22	23	24	25	26	27	28	29	30				
Dec	1	2	3	4	5	6	7	8	9	10	11	12	13	14	15	16	17
	18	19	20	21	22	23	24	25	26	27	28	29	30	31			

Seasonal Bucket List

Field Trip Planner

January	February	March

April	May	June

July	August	September

October	November	December
F? – 10/6 10/9		

Reading Record

Student

Title	Author	Pages

Time Tracker

Goals

Chore Chart

Name ______________________

Chore	S	M	T	W	T	F	S
	☐	☐	☐	☐	☐	☐	☐
	☐	☐	☐	☐	☐	☐	☐
	☐	☐	☐	☐	☐	☐	☐
	☐	☐	☐	☐	☐	☐	☐
	☐	☐	☐	☐	☐	☐	☐
	☐	☐	☐	☐	☐	☐	☐
	☐	☐	☐	☐	☐	☐	☐
	☐	☐	☐	☐	☐	☐	☐

Checklist

Chore	S	M	T	W	T	F	S
	☐	☐	☐	☐	☐	☐	☐
	☐	☐	☐	☐	☐	☐	☐
	☐	☐	☐	☐	☐	☐	☐
	☐	☐	☐	☐	☐	☐	☐
	☐	☐	☐	☐	☐	☐	☐
	☐	☐	☐	☐	☐	☐	☐
	☐	☐	☐	☐	☐	☐	☐
	☐	☐	☐	☐	☐	☐	☐

Checklist

Chore Chart

Name ______________________

Chore	S	M	T	W	T	F	S
	☐	☐	☐	☐	☐	☐	☐
	☐	☐	☐	☐	☐	☐	☐
	☐	☐	☐	☐	☐	☐	☐
	☐	☐	☐	☐	☐	☐	☐
	☐	☐	☐	☐	☐	☐	☐
	☐	☐	☐	☐	☐	☐	☐
	☐	☐	☐	☐	☐	☐	☐
	☐	☐	☐	☐	☐	☐	☐

Checklist

Chore	S	M	T	W	T	F	S
	☐	☐	☐	☐	☐	☐	☐
	☐	☐	☐	☐	☐	☐	☐
	☐	☐	☐	☐	☐	☐	☐
	☐	☐	☐	☐	☐	☐	☐
	☐	☐	☐	☐	☐	☐	☐
	☐	☐	☐	☐	☐	☐	☐
	☐	☐	☐	☐	☐	☐	☐
	☐	☐	☐	☐	☐	☐	☐

Chore Chart

Name ______________________

Chore	S	M	T	W	T	F	S
	☐	☐	☐	☐	☐	☐	☐
	☐	☐	☐	☐	☐	☐	☐
	☐	☐	☐	☐	☐	☐	☐
	☐	☐	☐	☐	☐	☐	☐
	☐	☐	☐	☐	☐	☐	☐
	☐	☐	☐	☐	☐	☐	☐
	☐	☐	☐	☐	☐	☐	☐
	☐	☐	☐	☐	☐	☐	☐

Checklist

Chore	S	M	T	W	T	F	S
	☐	☐	☐	☐	☐	☐	☐
	☐	☐	☐	☐	☐	☐	☐
	☐	☐	☐	☐	☐	☐	☐
	☐	☐	☐	☐	☐	☐	☐
	☐	☐	☐	☐	☐	☐	☐
	☐	☐	☐	☐	☐	☐	☐
	☐	☐	☐	☐	☐	☐	☐
	☐	☐	☐	☐	☐	☐	☐

Checklist

Chore Chart

Name ______________________

Chore	S	M	T	W	T	F	S
	☐	☐	☐	☐	☐	☐	☐
	☐	☐	☐	☐	☐	☐	☐
	☐	☐	☐	☐	☐	☐	☐
	☐	☐	☐	☐	☐	☐	☐
	☐	☐	☐	☐	☐	☐	☐
	☐	☐	☐	☐	☐	☐	☐
	☐	☐	☐	☐	☐	☐	☐
	☐	☐	☐	☐	☐	☐	☐

Checklist

Chore	S	M	T	W	T	F	S
	☐	☐	☐	☐	☐	☐	☐
	☐	☐	☐	☐	☐	☐	☐
	☐	☐	☐	☐	☐	☐	☐
	☐	☐	☐	☐	☐	☐	☐
	☐	☐	☐	☐	☐	☐	☐
	☐	☐	☐	☐	☐	☐	☐
	☐	☐	☐	☐	☐	☐	☐
	☐	☐	☐	☐	☐	☐	☐

Checklist

Daily Plan

STUDENT VERSION

Student ______________________ Date ______________

Checklist					
Course	M	T	W	T	F
	☐	☐	☐	☐	☐
	☐	☐	☐	☐	☐
	☐	☐	☐	☐	☐
	☐	☐	☐	☐	☐
	☐	☐	☐	☐	☐
	☐	☐	☐	☐	☐
	☐	☐	☐	☐	☐
	☐	☐	☐	☐	☐
	☐	☐	☐	☐	☐
	☐	☐	☐	☐	☐
	☐	☐	☐	☐	☐
	☐	☐	☐	☐	☐

Schedule	
Time	

Activities

Daily Plan

STUDENT VERSION

Student ______________________ Date ______________

Checklist					
Course	M	T	W	T	F
	☐	☐	☐	☐	☐
	☐	☐	☐	☐	☐
	☐	☐	☐	☐	☐
	☐	☐	☐	☐	☐
	☐	☐	☐	☐	☐
	☐	☐	☐	☐	☐
	☐	☐	☐	☐	☐
	☐	☐	☐	☐	☐
	☐	☐	☐	☐	☐
	☐	☐	☐	☐	☐
	☐	☐	☐	☐	☐
	☐	☐	☐	☐	☐

Schedule	
Time	

Activities

* To print additional copies for student use, please visit www.homeschool.com/free-stuff/planner"

Daily Plan

STUDENT VERSION

Student ______________________ Date ____________

Checklist

Course	M	T	W	T	F
	☐	☐	☐	☐	☐
	☐	☐	☐	☐	☐
	☐	☐	☐	☐	☐
	☐	☐	☐	☐	☐
	☐	☐	☐	☐	☐
	☐	☐	☐	☐	☐
	☐	☐	☐	☐	☐
	☐	☐	☐	☐	☐
	☐	☐	☐	☐	☐
	☐	☐	☐	☐	☐
	☐	☐	☐	☐	☐
	☐	☐	☐	☐	☐

Schedule

Time	

Activities

* To print additional copies for student use, please visit www.homeschool.com/free-stuff/planner"

Notes

Gratitude List

I'M THANKFUL FOR:

Goal setting

Quarterly Goals

Student

Year

Academics

Character/Spiritual

Other

Quarterly Goals

Student ______________________ Year ____________

Academics

Character/Spiritual

Other

Quarterly Goals

Student

Year

Academics

Character/Spiritual

Other

Quarterly Goals

Student

Year

Academics

Character/Spiritual

Other

Monthly Work Goals

Primary

Secondary

Resources Needed

Section 2

Vacation or Staycation Ideas

THINGS TO DO

What/Where to eat

What to pack/prepare

Remember

Due Dates

Reason	Date to remember

Year Planner

Month ____________________ Year ____________

Sun	Mon	Tues	Wed	Thurs	Fri	Sat

Password Log

Site	Username	Password

Project Planner

Step 1

Step 2

Step 3

Step 4

Project Planner Shopping List

Brainstorm

Brainstorm

Weekly Plans

36 weeks

Weekly Plan

Week

Monday	Tuesday	Wednesday

Weekly Plan

Thursday	Friday

Notes

Weekly Plan

Week

Monday	Tuesday	Wednesday

Weekly Plan

Thursday	Friday

Notes

Weekly Plan

Week

Monday	Tuesday	Wednesday

Weekly Plan

Thursday	Friday

Notes

Weekly Plan

Week

Monday	Tuesday	Wednesday

Weekly Plan

Thursday	Friday

Notes

Weekly Plan

Week

Monday	Tuesday	Wednesday

Weekly Plan

Thursday	Friday

Notes

Weekly Plan

Week

Monday	Tuesday	Wednesday

Weekly Plan

Notes

Thursday	Friday

Weekly Plan

Week

Monday	Tuesday	Wednesday

Weekly Plan

Thursday	Friday

Notes

Weekly Plan

Week

Monday	Tuesday	Wednesday

Weekly Plan

Thursday	Friday

Notes

Weekly Plan

Week

Monday	Tuesday	Wednesday

Weekly Plan

Thursday	Friday

Notes

Weekly Plan

Week

Monday	Tuesday	Wednesday

Weekly Plan

Thursday	Friday

Notes

Weekly Plan

Week

Monday	Tuesday	Wednesday

Weekly Plan

Thursday	Friday

Notes

Weekly Plan

Week

Monday	Tuesday	Wednesday

Weekly Plan

Thursday	Friday

Notes

Weekly Plan

Week

Monday	Tuesday	Wednesday

Weekly Plan

Thursday	Friday

Notes

Weekly Plan

Week

Monday	Tuesday	Wednesday

Weekly Plan

Thursday	Friday

Notes

Weekly Plan

Week

Monday	Tuesday	Wednesday

Weekly Plan

Thursday	Friday

Notes

Weekly Plan

Week

Monday	Tuesday	Wednesday

Weekly Plan

Thursday	Friday

Notes

Weekly Plan

Week

Monday	Tuesday	Wednesday

Weekly Plan

Thursday	Friday

Notes

Weekly Plan

Week

Monday	Tuesday	Wednesday

Weekly Plan

Thursday	Friday

Notes

Weekly Plan

Week

Monday	Tuesday	Wednesday

Weekly Plan

Thursday	Friday

Notes

Weekly Plan

Week

Monday	Tuesday	Wednesday

Weekly Plan

Thursday	Friday

Notes

Weekly Plan

Week

Monday	Tuesday	Wednesday

Weekly Plan

Thursday	Friday

Notes

Weekly Plan

Week

Monday	Tuesday	Wednesday

Weekly Plan

Thursday	Friday

Notes

Weekly Plan

Week

Monday	Tuesday	Wednesday

Weekly Plan

Thursday	Friday

Notes

Weekly Plan

Week

Monday	Tuesday	Wednesday

Weekly Plan

Thursday	Friday

Notes

Weekly Plan

Week

Monday	Tuesday	Wednesday

Weekly Plan

Notes

Thursday	Friday

Weekly Plan

Week

Monday	Tuesday	Wednesday

Weekly Plan

Thursday	Friday

Notes

Weekly Plan

Week

Monday	Tuesday	Wednesday

Weekly Plan

Thursday	Friday

Notes

Weekly Plan

Week

Monday	Tuesday	Wednesday

Weekly Plan

Thursday	Friday

Notes

Weekly Plan

Week

Monday	Tuesday	Wednesday

Weekly Plan

Thursday	Friday

Notes

Weekly Plan

Week

Monday	Tuesday	Wednesday

Weekly Plan

Thursday	Friday

Notes

Weekly Plan

Week

Monday	Tuesday	Wednesday

Weekly Plan

Thursday	Friday

Notes

Weekly Plan

Week

Monday	Tuesday	Wednesday

Weekly Plan

Thursday	Friday

Notes

Weekly Plan

Week

Monday	Tuesday	Wednesday

Weekly Plan

Thursday	Friday

Notes

Weekly Plan

Week

Monday	Tuesday	Wednesday

Weekly Plan

Thursday	Friday

Notes

Weekly Plan

Week

Monday	Tuesday	Wednesday

Weekly Plan

Thursday	Friday

Notes

Weekly Plan

Week

Monday	Tuesday	Wednesday

Weekly Plan

Thursday	Friday

Notes

Weekly Meal Plan

36 weeks

Weekly Meal Plan

	Breakfast	Lunch
Sunday		
Monday		
Tuesday		
Wednesday		
Thursday		
Friday		
Saturday		

Weekly Meal Plan

Supper	Snacks

Shopping

Weekly Meal Plan

	Breakfast	Lunch
Sunday		
Monday		
Tuesday		
Wednesday		
Thursday		
Friday		
Saturday		

Weekly Meal Plan

Supper	Snacks

Shopping

Weekly Meal Plan

	Breakfast	Lunch
Sunday		
Monday		
Tuesday		
Wednesday		
Thursday		
Friday		
Saturday		

Weekly Meal Plan

Supper	Snacks

Shopping

Weekly Meal Plan

	Breakfast	Lunch
Sunday		
Monday		
Tuesday		
Wednesday		
Thursday		
Friday		
Saturday		

Weekly Meal Plan

Supper	Snacks

Shopping

Weekly Meal Plan

	Breakfast	Lunch
Sunday		
Monday		
Tuesday		
Wednesday		
Thursday		
Friday		
Saturday		

Weekly Meal Plan

Supper	Snacks

Shopping

Weekly Meal Plan

	Breakfast	Lunch
Sunday		
Monday		
Tuesday		
Wednesday		
Thursday		
Friday		
Saturday		

Weekly Meal Plan

Supper	Snacks

Shopping

Weekly Meal Plan

	Breakfast	Lunch
Sunday		
Monday		
Tuesday		
Wednesday		
Thursday		
Friday		
Saturday		

Weekly Meal Plan

Supper	Snacks

Shopping

Weekly Meal Plan

	Breakfast	Lunch
Sunday		
Monday		
Tuesday		
Wednesday		
Thursday		
Friday		
Saturday		

Weekly Meal Plan

Supper	Snacks

Shopping

Weekly Meal Plan

	Breakfast	Lunch
Sunday		
Monday		
Tuesday		
Wednesday		
Thursday		
Friday		
Saturday		

Weekly Meal Plan

Supper	Snacks

Shopping

Weekly Meal Plan

	Breakfast	Lunch
Sunday		
Monday		
Tuesday		
Wednesday		
Thursday		
Friday		
Saturday		

Weekly Meal Plan

Supper	Snacks

Shopping

Weekly Meal Plan

	Breakfast	Lunch
Sunday		
Monday		
Tuesday		
Wednesday		
Thursday		
Friday		
Saturday		

Weekly Meal Plan

Supper	Snacks

Shopping

Weekly Meal Plan

	Breakfast	Lunch
Sunday		
Monday		
Tuesday		
Wednesday		
Thursday		
Friday		
Saturday		

Weekly Meal Plan

Supper	Snacks

Shopping

Weekly Meal Plan

	Breakfast	Lunch
Sunday		
Monday		
Tuesday		
Wednesday		
Thursday		
Friday		
Saturday		

Weekly Meal Plan

Supper	Snacks

Shopping

Weekly Meal Plan

	Breakfast	Lunch
Sunday		
Monday		
Tuesday		
Wednesday		
Thursday		
Friday		
Saturday		

Weekly Meal Plan

Supper	Snacks

Shopping

Weekly Meal Plan

	Breakfast	Lunch
Sunday		
Monday		
Tuesday		
Wednesday		
Thursday		
Friday		
Saturday		

Weekly Meal Plan

Supper	Snacks

Shopping

Weekly Meal Plan

	Breakfast	Lunch
Sunday		
Monday		
Tuesday		
Wednesday		
Thursday		
Friday		
Saturday		

Weekly Meal Plan

Supper	Snacks

Shopping

Weekly Meal Plan

	Breakfast	Lunch
Sunday		
Monday		
Tuesday		
Wednesday		
Thursday		
Friday		
Saturday		

Weekly Meal Plan

Supper	Snacks

Shopping

Weekly Meal Plan

	Breakfast	Lunch
Sunday		
Monday		
Tuesday		
Wednesday		
Thursday		
Friday		
Saturday		

Weekly Meal Plan

Supper	Snacks

Shopping

Weekly Meal Plan

	Breakfast	Lunch
Sunday		
Monday		
Tuesday		
Wednesday		
Thursday		
Friday		
Saturday		

Weekly Meal Plan

Supper	Snacks

Shopping

Weekly Meal Plan

	Breakfast	Lunch
Sunday		
Monday		
Tuesday		
Wednesday		
Thursday		
Friday		
Saturday		

Weekly Meal Plan

Supper	Snacks

Shopping

Weekly Meal Plan

	Breakfast	Lunch
Sunday		
Monday		
Tuesday		
Wednesday		
Thursday		
Friday		
Saturday		

Weekly Meal Plan

Supper	Snacks

Shopping

Weekly Meal Plan

	Breakfast	Lunch
Sunday		
Monday		
Tuesday		
Wednesday		
Thursday		
Friday		
Saturday		

Weekly Meal Plan

Supper	Snacks

Shopping

Weekly Meal Plan

	Breakfast	Lunch
Sunday		
Monday		
Tuesday		
Wednesday		
Thursday		
Friday		
Saturday		

Weekly Meal Plan

Supper	Snacks

Shopping

Weekly Meal Plan

	Breakfast	Lunch
Sunday		
Monday		
Tuesday		
Wednesday		
Thursday		
Friday		
Saturday		

Weekly Meal Plan

Supper	Snacks

Shopping

Weekly Meal Plan

	Breakfast	Lunch
Sunday		
Monday		
Tuesday		
Wednesday		
Thursday		
Friday		
Saturday		

Weekly Meal Plan

Supper	Snacks

Shopping

Weekly Meal Plan

	Breakfast	Lunch
Sunday		
Monday		
Tuesday		
Wednesday		
Thursday		
Friday		
Saturday		

Weekly Meal Plan

Supper	Snacks

Shopping

Weekly Meal Plan

	Breakfast	Lunch
Sunday		
Monday		
Tuesday		
Wednesday		
Thursday		
Friday		
Saturday		

Weekly Meal Plan

Supper	Snacks

Shopping

Weekly Meal Plan

	Breakfast	Lunch
Sunday		
Monday		
Tuesday		
Wednesday		
Thursday		
Friday		
Saturday		

Weekly Meal Plan

Supper	Snacks

Shopping

Weekly Meal Plan

	Breakfast	Lunch
Sunday		
Monday		
Tuesday		
Wednesday		
Thursday		
Friday		
Saturday		

Weekly Meal Plan

Supper	Snacks

Shopping

Weekly Meal Plan

	Breakfast	Lunch
Sunday		
Monday		
Tuesday		
Wednesday		
Thursday		
Friday		
Saturday		

Weekly Meal Plan

Supper	Snacks

Shopping

Weekly Meal Plan

	Breakfast	Lunch
Sunday		
Monday		
Tuesday		
Wednesday		
Thursday		
Friday		
Saturday		

Weekly Meal Plan

Supper	Snacks

Shopping

Weekly Meal Plan

	Breakfast	Lunch
Sunday		
Monday		
Tuesday		
Wednesday		
Thursday		
Friday		
Saturday		

Weekly Meal Plan

Supper	Snacks

Shopping

Weekly Meal Plan

	Breakfast	Lunch
Sunday		
Monday		
Tuesday		
Wednesday		
Thursday		
Friday		
Saturday		

Weekly Meal Plan

Supper	Snacks

Shopping

Weekly Meal Plan

	Breakfast	Lunch
Sunday		
Monday		
Tuesday		
Wednesday		
Thursday		
Friday		
Saturday		

Weekly Meal Plan

Supper	Snacks

Shopping

Weekly Meal Plan

	Breakfast	Lunch
Sunday		
Monday		
Tuesday		
Wednesday		
Thursday		
Friday		
Saturday		

Weekly Meal Plan

Supper	Snacks

Shopping

Weekly Meal Plan

	Breakfast	Lunch
Sunday		
Monday		
Tuesday		
Wednesday		
Thursday		
Friday		
Saturday		

Weekly Meal Plan

Supper	Snacks

Shopping

2019 Calendar

January

S	M	T	W	T	F	S
30	31	1	2	3	4	5
6	7	8	9	10	11	12
13	14	15	16	17	18	19
20	21	22	23	24	25	26
27	28	29	30	31	1	2

February

S	M	T	W	T	F	S
27	28	29	30	31	1	2
3	4	5	6	7	8	9
10	11	12	13	14	15	16
17	18	19	20	21	22	23
24	25	26	27	28	1	2

March

S	M	T	W	T	F	S
24	25	26	27	28	1	2
3	4	5	6	7	8	9
10	11	12	13	14	15	16
17	18	19	20	21	22	23
24	25	26	27	28	29	30
31	1	2	3	4	5	6

April

S	M	T	W	T	F	S
31	1	2	3	4	5	6
7	8	9	10	11	12	13
14	15	16	17	18	19	20
21	22	23	24	25	26	27
28	29	30	1	2	3	4

May

S	M	T	W	T	F	S
28	29	30	1	2	3	4
5	6	7	8	9	10	11
12	13	14	15	16	17	18
19	20	21	22	23	24	25
26	27	28	29	30	31	1

June

S	M	T	W	T	F	S
26	27	28	29	30	31	1
2	3	4	5	6	7	8
9	10	11	12	13	14	15
16	17	18	19	20	21	22
23	24	25	26	27	28	29
30	1	2	3	4	5	6

July

S	M	T	W	T	F	S
30	1	2	3	4	5	6
7	8	9	10	11	12	13
14	15	16	17	18	19	20
21	22	23	24	25	26	27
28	29	30	31	1	2	3

August

S	M	T	W	T	F	S
28	29	30	31	1	2	3
4	5	6	7	8	9	10
11	12	13	14	15	16	17
18	19	20	21	22	23	24
25	26	27	28	29	30	31

September

S	M	T	W	T	F	S
1	2	3	4	5	6	7
8	9	10	11	12	13	14
15	16	17	18	19	20	21
22	23	24	25	26	27	28
29	30	1	2	3	4	5

October

S	M	T	W	T	F	S
29	30	1	2	3	4	5
6	7	8	9	10	11	12
13	14	15	16	17	18	19
20	21	22	23	24	25	26
27	28	29	30	31	1	2

November

S	M	T	W	T	F	S
27	28	29	30	31	1	2
3	4	5	6	7	8	9
10	11	12	13	14	15	16
17	18	19	20	21	22	23
24	25	26	27	28	29	30

December

S	M	T	W	T	F	S
1	2	3	4	5	6	7
8	9	10	11	12	13	14
15	16	17	18	19	20	21
22	23	24	25	26	27	28
29	30	31	1	2	3	4

2020 Calendar

1 January

S	M	T	W	T	F	S
29	30	31	1	2	3	4
5	6	7	8	9	10	11
12	13	14	15	16	17	18
19	20	21	22	23	24	25
26	27	28	29	30	31	1

1 February

S	M	T	W	T	F	S
26	27	28	29	30	31	1
2	3	4	5	6	7	8
9	10	11	12	13	14	15
16	17	18	19	20	21	22
23	24	25	26	27	28	29

1 March

S	M	T	W	T	F	S
1	2	3	4	5	6	7
8	9	10	11	12	13	14
15	16	17	18	19	20	21
22	23	24	25	26	27	28
29	30	31	1	2	3	4

1 April

S	M	T	W	T	F	S
29	30	31	1	2	3	4
5	6	7	8	9	10	11
12	13	14	15	16	17	18
19	20	21	22	23	24	25
26	27	28	29	30	1	2

1 May

S	M	T	W	T	F	S
26	27	28	29	30	1	2
3	4	5	6	7	8	9
10	11	12	13	14	15	16
17	18	19	20	21	22	23
24	25	26	27	28	29	30
31	1	2	3	4	5	6

1 June

S	M	T	W	T	F	S
31	1	2	3	4	5	6
7	8	9	10	11	12	13
14	15	16	17	18	19	20
21	22	23	24	25	26	27
28	29	30	1	2	3	4

1 July

S	M	T	W	T	F	S
28	29	30	1	2	3	4
5	6	7	8	9	10	11
12	13	14	15	16	17	18
19	20	21	22	23	24	25
26	27	28	29	30	31	1

1 August

S	M	T	W	T	F	S
26	27	28	29	30	31	1
2	3	4	5	6	7	8
9	10	11	12	13	14	15
16	17	18	19	20	21	22
23	24	25	26	27	28	29
30	31	1	2	3	4	5

1 September

S	M	T	W	T	F	S
30	31	1	2	3	4	5
6	7	8	9	10	11	12
13	14	15	16	17	18	19
20	21	22	23	24	25	26
27	28	29	30	1	2	3

1 October

S	M	T	W	T	F	S
27	28	29	30	1	2	3
4	5	6	7	8	9	10
11	12	13	14	15	16	17
18	19	20	21	22	23	24
25	26	27	28	29	30	31

1 November

S	M	T	W	T	F	S
1	2	3	4	5	6	7
8	9	10	11	12	13	14
15	16	17	18	19	20	21
22	23	24	25	26	27	28
29	30	1	2	3	4	5

1 December

S	M	T	W	T	F	S
29	30	1	2	3	4	5
6	7	8	9	10	11	12
13	14	15	16	17	18	19
20	21	22	23	24	25	26
27	28	29	30	31	1	2

64774394R00106

Made in the USA
Columbia, SC
12 July 2019